MAX
VERSTAPPEN

Racing Beyond Limits

A BOIGRAPHY

Joshua R. Mason

1

Max Verstappen: A Biography

MAX
VERSTAPPEN

Racing Beyond Limits

A BOIGRAPHY

Joshua R. Mason

Table of Contents

Introduction

In the high-octane world of Formula One, where speed, precision, and nerve define the difference between victory and defeat, one name stands out as a beacon of excellence and determination. This book delves into the remarkable journey of Max Verstappen, a driver whose life story transcends the racetrack, encompassing triumphs, challenges, and a legacy that inspires far beyond the realm of motorsport.

Verstappen's rise from a young karting prodigy to a Formula One world champion is a narrative of passion, perseverance, and an unyielding pursuit of greatness. His journey is a testament to the power of ambition, hard work, and the unwavering belief in the ability to overcome obstacles on the path to achieving dreams.

Beyond the roar of engines and the frenzy of competition, this book aims to uncover the multifaceted dimensions that shape Max Verstappen's identity. From his aggressive driving style and tactical finesse to his contributions off the track that extend to safety advocacy, environmental consciousness, and philanthropy, Verstappen's impact resonates far beyond the laps he completes.

As we navigate the chapters that unfold, we will explore the moments that have defined Max Verstappen's career – the spectacular victories that ignited his ascent, the setbacks that tested his resilience, and the fierce rivalries that have electrified racetracks around the world. Through insights from engineers, teammates, and rivals, we gain a comprehensive understanding of the qualities that make him a champion – both on and off the track

Chapter 1: In the Beginning

In the quiet town of Hasselt, Belgium, the distant echoes of engines roared through the air every weekend. It was here that Max Emilian Verstappen, born on September 30, 1997, was introduced to the world of racing. His father, Jos Verstappen, had been a Formula One driver himself, and his grandfather, Jan Verstappen, was a successful kart racer. Racing ran in Max's blood, and from a young age, it was clear that he was destined for greatness.

Max's early days were spent watching his father tear up the tracks, his eyes wide with fascination as the sleek cars sped by. He could barely contain his excitement, and every night, he dreamt of becoming a racer just like his dad. It was as if the engine's song whispered secrets to his heart, promising a destiny filled with speed and adrenaline.

As soon as Max could walk, he was drawn to the family's collection of toy cars. He would push them around the house, creating intricate race scenarios in his mind. Jos noticed his son's fascination and decided to nurture it. At the tender age of four, Max was gifted a kart, a tiny machine that would become the vessel of his dreams.

The karting track became Max's second home. His tiny hands gripped the steering wheel, his feet barely reaching the pedals, but his determination far exceeded his physical size. Jos watched with pride as Max zipped around the track, his driving skills beyond his years. Even at that age, Max displayed a natural understanding of racing lines and a fearlessness that left seasoned veterans in awe.

As the years went by, Max's talents blossomed. He progressed through various karting categories, leaving a trail of victories in his wake. His speed and precision were unmatched, and he quickly gained a reputation as a prodigious talent. But it wasn't just his skills that set him apart; it was his relentless work ethic and hunger to improve that truly defined him.

Jos played a pivotal role in Max's development, acting as both a mentor and a father figure. He guided Max through the intricacies of racing, teaching him the importance of patience, strategy, and mental fortitude. Max absorbed every word, determined to follow in his father's footsteps while also carving his own path.

By the time Max was a teenager, his talents had outgrown the confines of the karting track. It was clear that he needed a bigger stage to showcase his abilities. Formula One had always been the ultimate goal, the pinnacle of motorsport. Max's ascent through the junior formulae was nothing short of meteoric. He won championships, set records, and proved time and again that he was a force to be reckoned with.

The world took notice when Max made his Formula One debut in 2015 with Scuderia Toro Rosso. At just 17 years old, he became the youngest driver ever to start a Formula One race. The media was abuzz with skepticism and anticipation. Could someone so young handle the pressure and speed of the world's most prestigious racing series?

Max's debut race at the 2015 Australian Grand Prix silenced the doubters. He drove with a poise and maturity that belied his age, finishing in a remarkable seventh place and scoring points on his very first outing. The paddock was abuzz with praise, and Formula One had found its new sensation.

But it wasn't all smooth sailing. Max faced his fair share of challenges and setbacks. There were races where he had to battle mechanical failures and collisions. Yet, each setback only fueled his determination to succeed. Max's ability to learn from his mistakes and bounce back stronger became a hallmark of his character.

A defining moment came at the age of 18, when Verstappen clinched victory at the 2016 Spanish Grand Prix in his debut for Red Bull Racing. This victory etched his name in the annals of Formula One as the youngest-ever race winner and the trailblazing first Dutch driver to seize a Formula One Grand Prix victory.

He shares his world with a younger sister, Victoria. Max's upbringing was marked by his parents' separation, leading him to live with his father, while his sister resided with their mother. Max's family tapestry extends to three younger half-siblings from his father's side - a sister named Blue Jaye from a second marriage and a brother and sister, Jason Jaxx and Mila Faye, from his father's current marriage.

The Verstappen family's roots intertwine deeply with motorsports: Jos Verstappen, Max's father, is a renowned Dutch former Formula One driver, while his Belgian mother showcased her prowess in karting. Even Max's first cousin once removed, Anthony Kumpen, etched his name in endurance racing and holds the distinction of being a two-time NASCAR Whelen Euro Series champion. Anthony currently serves as the team manager for PK Carsport in the Euro Series.

Though his mother hails from Belgium and he was born there, Max chose to carry a Dutch racing license. His affinity for the Dutch identity stemmed from spending more time with his father, deeply involved in his karting pursuits, and growing up amidst a Dutch community in Maaseik, a Belgian town bordering the Netherlands. Max once quipped, "I actually only lived in Belgium to sleep, but during the day I went to the Netherlands and had my friends there too. I was raised as a Dutch person, and that's how I feel." In 2022, Max elaborated that he cherishes both sides of his heritage, finding himself a harmonious blend of Belgian and Dutch influences.

Chapter 2: F1 Debut and Breakthrough

Max Verstappen's journey to racing stardom ignited within the precincts of his home province, Limburg, Belgium. It was there that he made his inaugural strides in the Mini Junior championship, setting the stage for his future racing endeavors. In 2006, Verstappen's racing mettle continued to grow as he graduated to the Rotax Max Minimax class, a stepping stone that saw him claim victory in the Belgian championship. This taste of success only fueled his determination, propelling him to clinch the Dutch Minimax championship in 2007.

But it was in a CRG kart, a vehicle infused with both mechanics and family history, that Verstappen truly blossomed. The Dutch and Belgian Minimax championships fell under his dominion, alongside the coveted Belgian Cadet championship, painting a portrait of a rising champion. By 2009, Team Pex Racing became the canvas for Verstappen's talents, leading to the conquest of the Flemish Minimax championship and the Belgian KF5 championship.

The year 2010 marked Verstappen's foray into international karting. Under the banner of CRG's factory team, he etched his name into the annals of karting history. In a duel with the more experienced Alexander Albon, he secured second place at the KF3 World Cup. Yet, triumph was his in the WSK Euro Series and the WSK World Series, where he surpassed Robert Vişoiu. The trajectory of success continued in 2011, with Verstappen's victory in the WSK Euro Series, orchestrated by a Parilla-powered CRG. He further honed his skills in the KF2 and KZ2 classes as part of the Intrepid Driver Program, culminating in victory at the WSK Master Series in the KF2 class.

As the tapestry of Verstappen's racing career continued to unfurl, the end of 2012 marked a significant shift. A pivotal decision saw him bid farewell to Intrepid, setting the stage for a new chapter in his racing narrative. A brief interlude with CRG-built Zanardi karts followed, only to see Verstappen eventually make his triumphant return to the embrace of the factory CRG team. The racing arenas witnessed his relentless pursuit of excellence. In a fierce showdown at the SKUSA SuperNationals in the KZ2 class, Verstappen exhibited his prowess astride a CRG, finishing 21st. But it was in 2013 that Verstappen's brilliance reached its zenith, etching his name into the annals of motorsport history.

At the tender age of 15, Verstappen achieved what many could only dream of. The year 2013 witnessed the dawn of an unprecedented era, with Verstappen seizing two European titles and a world title. The European and World KF and KZ championships became the canvas upon which Verstappen painted his legacy, leaving an indelible mark. Among his accomplishments was the 2013 World KZ championship, a triumph that resounded in Varennes-sur-Allier, France. A feat like no other, Verstappen ascended to the pinnacle, etching his name in the record books as the youngest driver ever to claim the coveted KZ world championship.

Verstappen's transition from karting to the realm of racing cars was a marked evolution in his journey. It was on a pivotal day, the 11th of October 2013, that the roar of engines replaced the silence of anticipation. The iconic Pembrey Circuit bore witness to Verstappen's inaugural encounter with a racing car, a Barazi-Epsilon FR2.0–10 Formula Renault machine. In an extraordinary display of determination, he completed an astounding 160 laps, igniting a passion that would blaze brightly in the years to come. The car was facilitated by the Dutch outfit MP Motorsport, a fitting alliance that foreshadowed Verstappen's meteoric rise.

His ascent through the ranks was marked by a series of tests and trials, each a stepping stone towards his destiny. Verstappen embarked on a series of tests with various Formula Renault 2.0 teams in 2013, probing the boundaries of his potential. Notably, he tested a Dallara F311 Formula 3 car orchestrated by Motopark Academy in December 2013, further expanding his horizons.

With each test, Verstappen etched his mark upon the track. A testament to his innate prowess, he outshone established names in the Formula Renault domain, leaving an indelible impression. At the Circuit Ricardo Tormo near Valencia, Verstappen's lap times eclipsed those of the seasoned Eddie Cheever III, a feat that resonated throughout the racing community.

The dawn of 2014 heralded a significant announcement – Verstappen's imminent racing debut in the Florida Winter Series, a non-championship event. The wheels of destiny were set in motion, and on the 5th of February, at the Palm Beach International Raceway, Verstappen soared to victory from pole position. The thrill of victory was matched by his triumph at Homestead–Miami Speedway, where he clinched his second victory in the series by a mere 0.004 seconds over Nicholas Latifi.

The resonance of Verstappen's single-seater debut reverberated through the corridors of motorsport. The FIA European Formula 3 Championship became his new arena, with Van Amersfoort Racing as his chosen allies. Aged just 16, Verstappen achieved the remarkable feat of securing a record six consecutive victories, further underlining his prodigious talent. With a record-breaking tally of ten victories and a journey punctuated by highs and lows, he finished third overall, an accomplishment that solidified his status as a force to be reckoned with on the international racing stage.

The world of Formula One awaited Max Verstappen with a mix of anticipation and skepticism. He was just a 17-year-old when he stepped onto the grid with Scuderia Toro Rosso, a fresh face in a realm dominated by seasoned racers. The paddock hummed with speculation – could this teenager truly hold his own in the pinnacle of motorsport?

His debut race at the 2015 Australian Grand Prix was a revelation. Amid the fierce competition, Max showcased a level of maturity that defied his age. Not only did he finish the race, but he also secured a commendable seventh place, earning precious points. As his rivals and observers took note, it was evident that Max Verstappen was no ordinary rookie.

As the season unfolded, Max's performances continued to defy expectations. He consistently outshone his more experienced teammate, demonstrating a unique fearlessness on the track. But it was the 2016 Spanish Grand Prix that would etch his name in the annals of Formula One history forever. Red Bull Racing, recognizing his potential, called Max up mid-season. The Spanish Grand Prix arrived, accompanied by rain and chaos. A first-lap collision between the Mercedes drivers presented a rare opportunity, and Max seized it with both hands.

As raindrops kissed the asphalt, Max's instincts guided him. He gambled on wet tires at precisely the right moment, a decision that would differentiate him from the pack. In the rain-soaked mayhem, he danced with his car, pushing the limits of control. Max's audacious overtakes painted a masterpiece on the wet canvas of the track, leaving fans and commentators stunned.

Chapter 3: Starting Years

In the realm of motorsport, where precision and speed intertwine, history is often scripted by those who dare to push the boundaries of age and possibility. A name that reverberates with this audacity is Max Emilian Verstappen, a prodigious talent whose journey from karting to the pinnacle of Formula One has been nothing short of extraordinary.

The stage was set at the illustrious 2014 Japanese Grand Prix, a pivotal juncture that would ultimately set the trajectory of Verstappen's career. In a move that would foreshadow his imminent full-time role with Toro Rosso in the forthcoming 2015 season, Verstappen took to the track, replacing the experienced Jean-Éric Vergne during the first practice session. Aged a mere 17 years and three days, this audacious participation not only heralded his readiness for Formula One but also etched his name into the annals of racing history as the youngest person ever to partake in a Formula One race weekend.

As the journey unfolded, Verstappen's story intertwined with the renowned Red Bull Junior Team. The year 2014 not only marked this strategic alliance but also witnessed Verstappen's foray into the Formula Renault 3.5 car arena through a series of tests that demonstrated his innate prowess. Amidst these exciting developments, the allure of Mercedes beckoned, presenting Verstappen with an invitation to join their prestigious driver development program, an embodiment of his prodigious potential.

The stage was now set for Verstappen's grand entrance onto the Formula One circuit. The dawn of the 2015 season marked the realization of a dream as he embarked on his full-time journey with Scuderia Toro Rosso. Amidst the iconic backdrop of the 2015 Australian Grand Prix, Verstappen's presence became a seismic event. In a pairing with Carlos Sainz, he stepped into the limelight as part of Toro Rosso's race driver lineup, making his Grand Prix debut as a full-time driver at the tender age of 17 years and 166 days. This audacious move not only defied conventional wisdom but also eclipsed the existing records, most notably Jaime Alguersuari's, by an astonishing margin of nearly two years.

The inaugural race, however, unfolded as a bittersweet chapter in Verstappen's journey. Running in points-scoring positions, the unexpected specter of an engine failure forced him into an untimely retirement. It was a reminder that even the most audacious aspirations are subject to the capricious nature of racing. Yet, Verstappen's resilience and resolve were steadfast.

The Malaysian Grand Prix emerged as the catalyst that crystallized his prowess on the Formula One stage. Qualifying an impressive sixth and navigating the race to secure seventh place, Verstappen catapulted himself into the ranks of Formula One point scorers. At just 17 years and 180 days, he seized the record for the youngest driver to accrue World Championship points, an accomplishment that resonated far beyond the realm of racing.

Undeterred by adversity, Verstappen's trajectory continued to ascend. Throughout the 2015 season, he showcased his tenacity by consistently finishing in the points. It was in Hungary that he demonstrated his mettle, claiming a notable fourth-place finish—an achievement that underscored his growing prowess on the track. He replicated this triumph at the United States Grand Prix, cementing his status as a formidable contender. The culmination of the season was marked by a triumphant appearance at the FIA Prize Giving

Ceremony. In a moment of affirmation, Verstappen received three prestigious awards: "Rookie of the Year," a testament to his meteoric rise; "Personality of the Year," an acknowledgment of his vibrant presence both on and off the track; and "Action of the Year," a well-deserved recognition for his audacious overtaking maneuver on Felipe Nasr at the daunting Blanchimont corner during the Belgian Grand Prix.

With the dawn of the 2016 season, Verstappen's journey took another turn, as he resumed his position at Toro Rosso alongside Carlos Sainz. The opening race in Australia saw him qualify an impressive fifth, yet it was marred by a tense encounter with his teammate. Frustration simmered as Verstappen found himself trailing Sainz on the track. Radio calls to his team unveiled his exasperation, a window into the competitive intensity that drives him. However, in the latter stages of the race, a fateful contact with Sainz's car left both Toro Rosso drivers nursing their respective ambitions on the dusty asphalt, with Verstappen ultimately securing a tenth-place finish.

Amidst the challenges, Verstappen's unwavering commitment to his craft shone brightly. The Bahrain Grand Prix emerged as a turning point, showcasing Verstappen's ability to overcome adversity. Crossing the line in sixth place, he etched his name in the history books by securing Toro Rosso's first-ever points at the Sakhir circuit. This achievement not only attested to Verstappen's skill behind the wheel but also resonated as a testament to his ability to extract success from the crucible of competition.

Max Verstappen: A Biography

<u>Chapter 4: The Red Bull Era</u>

On the 5th of May, 2016, in the wake of the Russian Grand Prix, a seismic shift occurred in the world of Formula One as Red Bull Racing unveiled a pivotal decision. Max Verstappen, the rising star of motorsport, would ascend to the helm of their racing stable, replacing Daniil Kvyat from the Spanish Grand Prix onwards. In a move that reverberated across the racing community, Kvyat returned to Toro Rosso, paving the way for Verstappen's meteoric rise. The announcement bore the stamp of Christian Horner, Red Bull's Team Principal, who spoke of Verstappen's undeniable talent, underlining his impressive performance at Toro Rosso. Horner's declaration encapsulated the sentiment of the moment, "Max has proven to be an outstanding young talent... pleased to give him the opportunity to drive for Red Bull Racing."

The Spanish Grand Prix would become the
stage for Verstappen's astonishing debut as a
Red Bull Racing driver. Qualifying an
impressive fourth, he catapulted himself into the
heart of the action on race day. As the sun-
drenched Circuit de Barcelona-Catalunya
reverberated with the roar of engines,
Verstappen's star would shine brightly. Amidst
the chaos of the opening lap, marked by the
dramatic exit of Mercedes' Lewis Hamilton and
Nico Rosberg, Verstappen surged to second
place, nestled behind his teammate Daniel
Ricciardo. A strategic masterstroke vaulted him
to the forefront, as he adopted a two-stop
strategy compared to Ricciardo's three, allowing
him to seize the race lead. The young Dutchman
held his ground, fending off the advances of
Ferrari's Kimi Räikkönen in the closing stages
to secure a remarkable victory. In an instant,
Verstappen rewrote the annals of Formula One
history, unseating Sebastian Vettel as the
youngest driver ever to clinch a Formula One

Grand Prix, a feat achieved at a mere 18 years and 228 days.

Verstappen's transition to Red Bull Racing was marked by a cascade of stellar performances. His initial eight races with the team glittered with excellence, boasting an impressive six top-five finishes, including an astonishing four podium appearances. The motorsport world had borne witness to the meteoric ascent of a young racer who consistently delivered on the grandest stage of them all.

The 2016 season saw Max Verstappen not only settling into his new team but also mastering the art of consistency. His podium finishes and remarkable drives garnered attention, but it was his maiden victory with Red Bull Racing that left the paddock in awe.

The 2016 Spanish Grand Prix, the same race that had marked his historic debut win the previous year, now presented a different kind of challenge. Max approached the race with an air of determination, knowing that repeating his earlier victory would demand his very best. As the lights went out, he surged forward with the intensity of a charging bull.

In a thrilling battle, Max engaged in a strategic duel with Kimi Räikkönen's Ferrari. A high-speed clash with Kimi Räikkönen at the first corner ignited controversy, while a sequence of aggressive maneuvers involving Sebastian Vettel, Räikkönen, and Sergio Pérez set the tone for a fierce showdown. Verstappen's driving style attracted criticism, with Räikkönen ominously predicting the potential for a significant accident. Christian Horner acknowledged the fine line Verstappen was treading, describing his driving as "on the edge," while emphasizing the learning process that lay ahead. Lap after lap, he defended his position with unwavering resolve, showcasing his ability to remain unflappable under pressure. As the checkered flag waved, Max secured his first victory with Red Bull Racing. The roar of the crowd mixed with the jubilation in the team garage, painting a vivid picture of his triumph.

he 2016 Brazilian Grand Prix stands as an indelible chapter in Max Verstappen's racing journey, a testament to his tenacity and prowess under challenging conditions. As the rain-soaked Interlagos circuit hosted a thrilling spectacle, Verstappen's star would once again rise.

Qualifying in a formidable fourth position, Verstappen positioned himself for a race that would epitomize his dynamic skill set. However, the heavens unleashed their unpredictable deluge, rendering the track treacherous. Amidst the rain and uncertainty, Verstappen's race took a perilous turn on the main straight. A sudden loss of traction sent his car into a spine-tingling slide towards the barriers, a moment where the very limits of control were tested.

Yet, it was precisely in moments of adversity that Verstappen's brilliance shone most brightly. After an intermediate tyre change, the young Dutchman found himself in 16th place with a mere 15 laps remaining. The dwindling laps would become a canvas for Verstappen's masterful overtaking maneuvers. With a seemingly magnetic connection to the rain-slicked track, he carved his way through the field, overtaking competitors with the precision of an artist.

The crescendo of his race came in rapid succession, culminating in a breathtaking podium finish in third place. Verstappen's performance was nothing short of awe-inspiring. It earned him accolades from across the paddock, with rival team Mercedes' principal, Toto Wolff, dubbing the race "The Verstappen Show." Wolff's description was a fitting tribute to a driver who seemed to defy the laws of physics with his audacious moves, a display that bordered on the realm of redefining what was deemed possible on the track.

However, every narrative contains multiple perspectives. While Verstappen basked in well-deserved acclaim, he also encountered the critical gaze of a four-time world champion, Sebastian Vettel. In a late-race maneuver at the Junção corner, Verstappen's actions forced Vettel off the track, sparking controversy. Vettel's contention echoed in the corridors of the paddock, but the race stewards differed in their assessment. Their judgment prevailed, as no reprimand was deemed necessary, a decision that crystallized the complex interplay of competition and interpretation.

The rivalry with his teammate, Daniel Ricciardo, was an intriguing subplot of the Red Bull Racing era. Both drivers shared a mutual respect and a burning desire to outshine the other. The 2017 Azerbaijan Grand Prix epitomized the fierce competition between the two.

In a chaotic race, Max and Daniel found themselves entangled in a collision, a moment that could have torn the team apart. Instead, it became a crucible of character. Red Bull Racing's management held their breath, waiting for the aftermath of the incident. The drivers, however, displayed a remarkable maturity. They recognized that their rivalry should never endanger the team's success. This moment of sportsmanship solidified the bond between Max and Daniel and demonstrated their commitment to a greater cause.

From the Malaysian Grand Prix onward, Max Verstappen embarked on a remarkable ascent, etching his name in the annals of Formula One history with a series of extraordinary achievements. The turning point of his career would be marked by a cascade of triumphs that showcased his remarkable skill and unwavering determination.

On a historic day, just after celebrating his 20th birthday, Verstappen secured his second Formula One victory at the 2017 Malaysian Grand Prix. In a display of audacious brilliance, he surpassed the three-time champion Lewis Hamilton, seizing the lead in the race's early stages. The victory wasn't just a testament to his raw speed; it was a attestation to his burgeoning prowess as a strategist, a masterful navigator of the track's intricacies.

Verstappen's momentum carried him to the following race in Japan, where he held court with a commanding performance, securing a well-deserved second-place finish. The stage was set for him to further demonstrate his mettle at the United States Grand Prix. A podium finish seemed certain, with Verstappen crossing the line in third. However, a post-race evaluation cast a shadow over his achievement.

His final-lap overtake on Kimi Räikkönen was ruled illegal, altering his classification to fourth. It was a reminder of the fine line between triumph and contention, a lesson that Verstappen embraced with humility.

The 2018 season brought a new set of challenges as Max navigated through technical difficulties and race incidents. His collision with Esteban Ocon after the Brazilian Grand Prix showcased the intensity of his emotions. Max's fiery post-race confrontation with Ocon echoed his father's own competitive spirit, a reminder that the passion for racing ran deep in his veins.

Verstappen's journey reached a crescendo in Mexico, a race etched in history for his exceptional performance. Mechanical issues may have cost him a pole position, but it didn't deter his determination. A bold start catapulted him into the lead, and Verstappen held his ground with unwavering focus. As he crossed

the finish line, the crowd erupted in jubilation –
he had secured his fifth career win and etched
his name in the annals of Formula One history.

The Brazilian Grand Prix showcased both
Verstappen's brilliance and the unpredictable
nature of racing. Dominating the track, he
executed stunning overtakes, leaving his rivals
in awe. Yet, a collision with Esteban Ocon
altered the trajectory of his victory. Despite the
setback, Verstappen's spirit remained unbroken
as he secured a hard-fought second place behind
Lewis Hamilton. The Abu Dhabi Grand Prix
marked the culmination of a remarkable season.
With another podium finish, Verstappen
demonstrated his consistency and unwavering
commitment to excellence. As the checkered
flag fell, he closed the chapter on a season that
had seen him triumph, stumble, and grow.

Off the track, Max's genuine demeanor and
approachability earned him a legion of fans. He
was often seen mingling with supporters,

signing autographs, and engaging in playful banter. He had the uncanny ability to make fans feel like they were part of his journey, a connection that went beyond the racetrack.

Chapter 5: The Rise of a Contender

The 2019 Formula One season marked a pivotal moment in Max Verstappen's career and in the history of the Red Bull Racing team. With the switch from Renault to Honda power units, the season was brimming with anticipation and excitement as the team aimed to redefine their position on the Formula One grid. Additionally, the departure of Daniel Ricciardo saw Verstappen joined by Pierre Gasly, setting the stage for a season of intense battles, triumphs, and challenges.

The season opener in Australia served as a tantalizing preview of what was to come. Verstappen's skill and determination were evident as he secured a commendable fourth-place qualification and ultimately clinched a well-deserved podium, finishing in third place.

This marked a significant milestone as it heralded the first podium finish for a Honda-powered driver since the 2008 British Grand Prix. As the Bahrain Grand Prix unfolded, Verstappen's competitive spirit was once again on display. He found himself on the cusp of another podium finish, but a late safety car intervention denied him the opportunity to overtake Charles Leclerc's faltering Ferrari. Despite the setback, Verstappen crossed the line in fourth place, showcasing his unwavering tenacity.

Verstappen's journey through the 2019 season was characterized by a series of remarkable performances. Notably, he secured fourth-place finishes in both the Chinese and Azerbaijan Grands Prix, showcasing his consistency in the midfield battles. The Spanish Grand Prix brought Verstappen back to the podium, as he demonstrated his skill and determination by clinching third place.

The prestigious Monaco Grand Prix unfolded with its characteristic blend of glamour and challenge. Verstappen's prowess was evident as he qualified in an impressive third place, positioning himself for a strong race. However, the intricacies of pit stops played a pivotal role. Verstappen's release into the path of Valtteri Bottas during the pit stops elevated him to second place, but a subsequent 5-second penalty ultimately pushed him down to fourth upon crossing the finish line.

The Canadian Grand Prix brought its own set of trials for Verstappen. An unfortunate red flag during the qualifying session disrupted his final lap, leading to an 11th-place qualification and a ninth-place start on the grid. Undeterred by the setback, Verstappen demonstrated his skill and determination, embarking on a stunning recovery to finish the race in fifth place.

Continuing on his trajectory of consistent performances, Verstappen secured a fourth-place finish in France. As the season reached Austria, Verstappen faced both challenges and triumphs. Starting from third on the grid, he endured a poor start that dropped him to eighth place. However, his relentless pursuit saw him navigate his way through the field, eventually passing Leclerc in a climactic battle for the lead with three laps to go. This monumental victory not only showcased Verstappen's prowess but also marked Honda's return to the winner's circle since 2006.

The British Grand Prix was a mixed bag for Verstappen. While running in third place, he became entangled in a collision with Sebastian Vettel, resulting in a spin into the gravel. Despite the setback, Verstappen showcased his resilience by recovering and crossing the finish line in fifth place.

The German Grand Prix provided yet another stage for Verstappen's meteoric rise. A poor start saw him initially fall behind, but as rain drenched the circuit, Verstappen's skills came to the fore. Benefiting from a crash by race leader Lewis Hamilton, Verstappen inherited the lead and expertly maneuvered through the changing conditions to secure his second victory of the season.

Hungary marked a monumental achievement for Verstappen as he clinched his maiden pole position. Leading for the majority of the race, he narrowly missed victory due to a late surge from Lewis Hamilton, who strategically gambled on fresh tires. Nonetheless, Verstappen's pole position and strong performance reaffirmed his position as a force to be reckoned with on the track.

The latter half of the season introduced changes to Verstappen's teammate lineup, with Alexander Albon replacing Pierre Gasly before the Belgian Grand Prix. Unfortunately, Verstappen faced a challenging race in Belgium as a collision with Kimi Räikkönen resulted in suspension damage, leading to his first retirement of the season. Italy posed a different kind of test, with Verstappen's car experiencing power loss during qualifying. Despite starting from the back of the grid due to penalties, Verstappen's unwavering determination saw him climb through the field to secure an eighth-place finish.

Verstappen's performance continued to impress with podium finishes in Singapore, Russia, and the United States. Mexico saw him secure pole position with a blistering lap, only to face a grid penalty for ignoring yellow flags. Despite starting further back, Verstappen showcased his skill by recovering to finish sixth. The United States Grand Prix witnessed Verstappen clinching third place, setting the stage for an electrifying performance in Brazil.

In Brazil, Verstappen stormed to his second career pole position, setting a new lap record. In a chaotic race marked by multiple incidents,

Verstappen executed bold overtakes and held off challenges, including a dramatic collision with Esteban Ocon while lapping him. Ultimately, Verstappen secured his third victory of the season, solidifying his status as a race-winning contender.

As the 2019 season drew to a close, Verstappen secured a second-place finish in Abu Dhabi, rounding out a season filled with podiums, pole positions, and thrilling battles on the track. His consistent performance and remarkable achievements earned him a third-place finish in the championship standings, amassing 278 points. With three race victories, nine podium finishes, two pole positions, and three fastest laps, Verstappen's journey through the 2019 season showcased his evolution into a dominant force in Formula One racing.

Chapter 6: A Season of Resilience and Triumph

The year 2020 marked a pivotal chapter in Max Verstappen's Formula One journey. With the challenges and uncertainties brought on by the global pandemic, the season promised to be unlike any other. As the lights went out in Australia, the anticipation was palpable, and Verstappen was prepared to continue his ascent in the world of motorsport. Verstappen's commitment to Red Bull was solidified with a contract extension that would see him in the driver's seat until the end of 2023. Armed with this renewed partnership, Verstappen faced the 2020 season with determination and resolve.

Verstappen's campaign began with the Australian Grand Prix, a race that had a rollercoaster journey even before the start. Amidst the growing concerns over the pandemic, the race weekend was dramatically canceled just hours before the first practice session. The season's opening was postponed, and the racing world was left in suspense.

Months later, As the engines roared to life at the 2020 Austrian Grand Prix, Verstappen's ambition was palpable. Starting from second on the grid, he was poised for a strong performance. However, fate had other plans. A flywheel-related issue triggered an electronic glitch within the power unit, leading to an early retirement from the race. It was a setback, but Verstappen's focus remained unwavering.

The Hungarian Grand Prix provided a dramatic turn of events. In wet conditions during the formation lap, Verstappen's car skidded and collided with the barriers. Undeterred, he displayed remarkable composure as he steered his damaged car back to the grid. The mechanics worked swiftly to mend the suspension, and Verstappen's determination paid off. Starting from seventh on the grid, he surged through the field to claim an impressive second-place finish.

Verstappen's triumphs continued as he secured victory at the 70th Anniversary Grand Prix at Silverstone. Starting from fourth on the grid, he navigated the challenges of the circuit with finesse, showcasing his ability to seize opportunities and emerge victorious.

Throughout the season, Verstappen's consistency and grit shone through. At the Spanish Grand Prix, he secured a second-place finish, adding to his tally of podiums. The Belgian Grand Prix saw him claim another podium finish in third place, reinforcing his position among the frontrunners. The Italian and Tuscan Grands Prix presented formidable challenges. A sequence of retirements dented Verstappen's campaign, momentarily pushing him back in the championship standings. Yet, his determination remained unyielding, and he demonstrated his resilience by bouncing back stronger.

The Russian Grand Prix witnessed Verstappen's relentless pursuit of excellence. Crossing the line in second place, he secured his seventh podium finish of the season, reaffirming his prowess on the track. The Eifel Grand Prix further showcased his skill as he secured second place after starting from third on the grid, accompanied by the fastest lap of the race.

Verstappen's journey continued with the Portuguese Grand Prix, where his unrelenting drive was evident. Though a challenging first lap saw him slip down the order, he mounted a remarkable recovery to secure third place and mark his 40th podium in Formula One. The Emilia Romagna Grand Prix offered a mix of promise and disappointment. Verstappen was on track for a podium finish, only to be thwarted by a sudden puncture that led to his fourth retirement of the season.

Beyond the racetrack, Verstappen found himself embroiled in a controversy. His comments during Free Practice for the Portuguese Grand Prix drew criticism for the use of inappropriate language. Verstappen promptly acknowledged the error in his choice of words, demonstrating his accountability and willingness to learn.

 The challenges posed by the pandemic and the dynamic nature of the season only fueled his determination to excel. With two race victories, eleven podium finishes, one pole position, and three fastest laps, Verstappen concluded the season in third place in the championship standings. Each race was a chapter in his story of resilience, grit, and relentless pursuit of excellence. As the racing world looked toward the future, Verstappen's legacy was firmly established, and his journey continued to inspire and captivate.

Chapter 7: Quest for the Championship

The dawn of the 2021 season marked a defining moment in Max Verstappen's career as he embarked on a journey that would culminate in the ultimate glory of a World Championship title. The racing world witnessed his exceptional talent, fierce determination, and unwavering resolve in a season that would etch his name in the annals of Formula One history.

The Bahrain Grand Prix set the stage for Verstappen's championship aspirations. Topping all practice sessions, he secured a career fourth pole position, a feat that underlined his prowess. The race unfolded as a fierce battle between Verstappen and his rival Lewis Hamilton. On lap 53, Verstappen's audacious move saw him overtake Hamilton, only to momentarily go off-track in the process.

Race control instructed him to relinquish the lead, and he ultimately finished second. The encounter showcased Verstappen's tenacity and hunger for victory.

At the Emilia Romagna Grand Prix, Verstappen faced a unique challenge. Starting from third on the grid, he was out-qualified by teammate Sergio Pérez for the first time since 2019. However, Verstappen's racecraft was on full display as he surged ahead to take the lead, exhibiting his ability to seize opportunities and dictate the pace of the race. The victory narrowed the championship gap to a single point, underlining the intensity of the battle that lay ahead.

The Portuguese Grand Prix saw Verstappen engaged in an epic duel with Hamilton. The two champions fiercely contested every inch of the track, with Verstappen ultimately finishing second. The Spanish Grand Prix intensified the rivalry, as a strategic two-stop strategy by

Hamilton allowed him to secure victory. Verstappen's second-place finish, coupled with the fastest lap, extended Hamilton's championship lead.

Monaco proved to be a turning point in the season. Verstappen's second-place qualification behind Charles Leclerc positioned him for victory after Leclerc's unfortunate pre-race mechanical failure. Verstappen commanded the race from the front, clinching victory and ascending to the top of the Drivers' Championship standings for the first time. It was a moment of profound significance in his journey.

The Azerbaijan Grand Prix brought its own share of drama. Despite Verstappen's early retirement due to a tire failure, a mistake by Hamilton enabled Verstappen to retain his championship lead. The French Grand Prix continued the seesaw battle between Verstappen and Hamilton. Verstappen's initial mistake allowed Hamilton to take the lead, but the Dutch driver orchestrated a stunning comeback, securing victory with a late overtake. The fastest lap point further bolstered his championship campaign.

The 2021 season continued to unfold as a thrilling saga of triumph, challenges, and fierce competition, with Max Verstappen demonstrating unparalleled resilience and determination in pursuit of his ultimate goal: the World Championship title. As the championship pendulum swung, Verstappen's journey remained as captivating as ever.

The Austrian Grand Prix marked a historic milestone in Verstappen's career. Securing pole position, he embarked on a dominating performance, leading every lap, setting the fastest lap, and clinching victory. This grand slam showcased his mastery of the track. Not only did he secure his first career grand slam, but he also became the youngest driver ever to do so. The victory was also the culmination of an extraordinary three-week stretch where he secured victories in three consecutive races, solidifying his place in Formula One history.

However, the racing gods had more twists in store. The British Grand Prix turned into a defining moment, as Verstappen's collision with Lewis Hamilton at Copse corner resulted in a jaw-dropping impact with the barrier. The high-speed crash sent shockwaves through the racing world. Verstappen's well-being remained a primary concern, and he underwent medical checks to ensure his safety. While Hamilton emerged victorious, the incident reduced Verstappen's championship lead to eight points, showcasing the fierce rivalry that had intensified throughout the season.

The Hungarian Grand Prix brought its own set of challenges. In a chaotic multi-car collision on the first lap, Verstappen's car suffered damage. Despite the setbacks, he pressed on, finishing tenth and eventually being promoted to ninth after Sebastian Vettel's disqualification. However, the race outcome played a pivotal role in allowing Hamilton to seize the championship lead.

The summer break served as a crucial juncture for Verstappen. The resumption of the season saw him continue to fight with unrelenting vigor. The Belgian Grand Prix saw Verstappen claim pole position ahead of George Russell and Hamilton. Despite the race being significantly affected by rain and limited to just a few laps, Verstappen's performance allowed him to retain his pole position, and half points were awarded. This narrowed the championship gap to just three points, setting the stage for an enthralling showdown.

The Dutch Grand Prix was a homecoming of sorts for Verstappen. Qualifying on pole, he held his ground against attacks from the Mercedes drivers, securing a victory that propelled him into the lead of the Drivers' Championship by a slim margin of three points.

The Russian Grand Prix presented Verstappen with yet another challenge, as a grid penalty forced him to start from the back. Undeterred, he carved his way through the field, finishing a commendable second after a strategic pit stop. The Turkish Grand Prix saw Verstappen battling changing conditions, finishing second behind Bottas. With Hamilton's finishing 5th position, Verstappen extended his lead in the championship by six points.

The United States Grand Prix served as a demonstration of Verstappen's unwavering pursuit of excellence. Claiming pole position by a margin of 0.209 seconds over Hamilton, Verstappen went on to win the race, extending his lead in the Drivers' Championship to twelve points. The victory was a statement of intent, a showcase of his skill, and a demonstration of his ability to perform under immense pressure.

As the season ventured into the 2021 Mexico City Grand Prix, Verstappen's battle against Hamilton intensified. Starting from the third position on the grid, he executed a masterful start to seize the lead from both Bottas and Hamilton into turn 1. Clinching victory, Verstappen widened the gap in the championship to a significant 19 points. Every race seemed to push the limits of both competitors, showcasing the true essence of motorsport rivalry.

The ultimate climax awaited at the Abu Dhabi Grand Prix. Verstappen and Hamilton entered the final round on equal points, with Verstappen leading due to a countback. The stage was set for a historic showdown, and the world watched with bated breath. Verstappen's journey was emblematic of his relentless pursuit of excellence, and the championship title was within his grasp.

Qualifying on pole by a substantial margin of nearly four-tenths of a second, Verstappen's race took an unexpected turn with a slow start off the line. He dropped to second place, with Hamilton leading the way. The championship hung in the balance, and the race itself was a roller-coaster of emotions.

A late safety car brought a dramatic twist, bringing Verstappen back into contention. With the resumption of the race, controversy ensued over the lapped cars allowed through. The tense battle extended beyond the track as the teams engaged in a protest and counter-arguments, leading to a post-race investigation.

Amid the intense scrutiny, Verstappen's determination shone. On the final lap of the race, he made a decisive move at turn 5 to overtake Hamilton, clinching victory and etching his name in the annals of Formula One history. The roar of the crowd, the thrill of the moment, and the weight of his accomplishment converged as Verstappen became the 34th Formula One World Drivers' Champion. The 2021 season will forever stand as a defining chapter in Verstappen's career, a reminder of the passion, rivalry, and unmatched pursuit of greatness that defines the world of Formula One.

Chapter 8: Struggles and Setbacks

Max Verstappen's journey to championship glory was a path filled with exhilarating triumphs and heart-wrenching setbacks. As he pursued his dream of becoming a Formula One world champion, he encountered obstacles that tested his mettle, shaped his character, and cemented his legacy as a true contender. Max Verstappen's journey to becoming a Formula One world champion was not a smooth ascent to glory. Alongside his remarkable triumphs, his path was littered with setbacks and challenges that tested his resilience, mental fortitude, and determination to conquer the highest echelons of motorsport.

The early stages of Max's career were characterized by rapid progress, but his baptism by fire in the world of Formula One was not

without its difficulties. The intensity of the
sport, the scrutiny from the media, and the
pressure to perform weighed heavily on his
young shoulders. The challenge wasn't just
about driving fast; it was about adapting to an
entirely new level of competition. As Max
navigated his rookie season, he encountered
adversities that cast a spotlight on his ability to
overcome adversity. The 2015 Belgian Grand
Prix saw him involved in a first-lap collision
that resulted in an early retirement. It was a
harsh introduction to the unforgiving nature of
Formula One racing, but Max's response was a
result of his determination. He emerged from
the experience with newfound wisdom,
resolving to learn from his mistakes.

The 2017 Chinese Grand Prix exposed Max to
the harsh realities of racing dynamics. A
collision with Ferrari's Sebastian Vettel led to a
post-race confrontation, highlighting the
emotional stakes at play. Max's fiery temper,
while a reflection of his passion, was a

challenge he needed to master. He recognized that the mental game of Formula One was as crucial as his driving skills.

The initial 14 races of the season were rife with challenges that put Verstappen's skills and patience to the test. Among these trials, retirements became a recurring theme, with seven of the races ending prematurely for him. Four of these retirements were attributed to mechanical issues, a harsh reminder of the inherent unpredictability of motorsport. The first lap collisions during the Spanish, Austrian, and Singapore Grands Prix further compounded Verstappen's difficulties. Despite the best efforts of both driver and team, circumstances beyond their control resulted in three races where Verstappen was unable to progress beyond the opening lap.

The 2018 Formula One season was a rollercoaster ride for Max Verstappen, marked by setbacks and challenges that put his resilience and determination to the test. Yet, amidst the turmoil, Verstappen's ability to bounce back showcased his growth as a driver and his unwavering commitment to success. The opening six races of the season proved to be a string of trials for Verstappen, each race presenting its own set of obstacles. From Australia to Monaco, he found himself entangled in incidents that hindered his progress and tested his mental fortitude.

In Australia, Verstappen's qualifying efforts placed him fourth, but a challenging start saw him slipping behind Kevin Magnussen. In his quest to regain his position, he found himself running wide multiple times, damaging his car and even spinning, which pushed him further down the order. Despite the difficulties, he displayed his resilience by clawing his way back to finish in sixth place. The Bahrain Grand Prix saw Verstappen's fortunes take a further dip. Qualifying 15th due to a crash during the session, he managed a commendable first lap, moving up the order and challenging Lewis Hamilton. However, an ill-fated overtake attempt resulted in a collision with Hamilton, puncturing his hopes and forcing him to retire from the race.

China's race offered a glimmer of hope as Verstappen battled back from a fifth-place qualifying to secure third on the opening lap. However, an incident involving Sebastian Vettel dropped him down the order, and a collision incurred a 10-second penalty. Yet, he fought back to secure fourth place, showcasing his determination even in the face of adversity.

In Azerbaijan, a teammate clash with Daniel Ricciardo resulted in a double retirement for Red Bull. Despite the setback, Verstappen refused to be defeated. In Spain, he secured his first podium of the season, finishing third. Though not without incident, as he made contact with Lance Stroll during the virtual safety car period. Monaco proved to be a defining moment in the season. A crash during practice forced Verstappen to start from the back of the grid. Despite the setback, he showcased his skill by overtaking six cars and securing two points with a ninth-place finish. The race highlighted his determination to make the best out of unfavorable circumstances.

The 2019 season, although marked by moments of brilliance, was defined by a level of consistency that was at times elusive. The Austrian Grand Prix bore witness to a heart-wrenching tire failure on the final lap while leading, robbing him of a victory that was within his grasp. The frustration was palpable, but Max's response was indicative of his unwavering spirit. He channeled his disappointment into determination, vowing to return stronger.

The 2020 season brought a unique set of challenges as the COVID-19 pandemic disrupted the world and Formula One as a whole. The uncertainties surrounding the schedule, the absence of fans, and the condensed calendar demanded adaptability. Max's ability to maintain focus and extract maximum performance from himself and his car was a challenge he met head-on.

The 2020 Formula One season brought a fresh set of challenges for Max Verstappen as he continued his journey with Red Bull Racing. While the season was marked by unprecedented circumstances due to the global pandemic, Verstappen's determination and resilience were put to the test as he navigated a series of highs and lows.

The season kicked off with the Austrian Grand Prix, where Verstappen started strong, securing a second-place starting position. However, his race was cut short by an unexpected flywheel-related problem that triggered an electronic issue within his power unit, forcing him to retire early. This early setback hinted at the hurdles Verstappen would face in the upcoming races.

The Hungarian Grand Prix saw Verstappen grappling with the treacherous conditions during the formation lap. Despite crashing on his way to the starting grid, he showcased strength and determination by driving the damaged car back to the grid. Although, his mechanics, the suspension of the car was repaired in record time. The race itself turned into a triumph of sorts as Verstappen charged from seventh place on the grid to secure an impressive second-place finish.

The Emilia Romagna Grand Prix served as a poignant example of the highs and lows Verstappen experienced during the season. Positioned to secure a promising second place due to Valtteri Bottas' ailing Mercedes, fate dealt him a cruel hand. A sudden puncture dashed his hopes of a podium finish, causing him to spin out and leading to his fourth retirement of the season. This unforeseen twist was a stark reminder of the unpredictable nature of motorsport, a reminder that Verstappen took in stride as he prepared for the challenges ahead.

However, adversity wasn't limited to the track. During Free Practice for the Portuguese Grand Prix, Verstappen found himself in a different kind of storm. Following a collision with Lance Stroll, his frustration led to a choice of words on the team radio that ignited controversy. His use of offensive language, including the terms "retard" and "mongol," drew criticism and condemnation from various quarters. Verstappen swiftly acknowledged his mistake, admitting that his word choices were inappropriate. The Mongolian government and the Mongol identity were among those urging an apology and action from the FIA.

These episodes underscored the multi-dimensional challenges that a modern Formula

One driver faces. The intensity of competition is accompanied by a spotlight that magnifies every action and word. Verstappen's willingness to take responsibility for his language and to learn from the incident demonstrated his maturity and humility.

Amidst these hurdles, Verstappen's determination remained unshakeable. He continued to prove his mettle on the track, securing podium finishes and making his mark on the championship battle. The resilience he displayed in the face of setbacks mirrored his growth as a driver and a person.

The 2020 season culminated in a third-place finish in the championship, with Verstappen amassing 214 points. His ability to secure two race victories, achieve eleven podium finishes, clinch one pole position, and set three fastest laps showcased his unwavering commitment to excellence. The setbacks he encountered only served to strengthen his resolve, highlighting his capacity to rise above challenges and emerge stronger.

The 2022 season marked a new chapter in Max's career, a season that would bring its own share of challenges. The pursuit of the championship became a high-stakes battle against time, as he sought to dethrone the reigning champion, Lewis Hamilton. The Red Bull RB18 was a competitive machine, but it was a duel against Mercedes that would define Max's year.

The Australian Grand Prix kicked off the season, and the rivalry between Max and Lewis intensified. Their battle on the track was fierce, characterized by close racing and strategic masterstrokes. The Bahrain Grand Prix saw them clash once again, showcasing the knife-edge balance between success and adversity.

But it was the Monaco Grand Prix that became a pivot point. The prestigious street circuit, known for its unforgiving nature, revealed a challenge Max couldn't overcome. In a tight qualifying session, Max's crash left him at the back of the grid. The race became an exercise in damage control, as he fought valiantly to salvage points. It was a stark reminder that even the most talented drivers could succumb to the unpredictable nature of racing.

The 2022 Azerbaijan Grand Prix further underscored the thin line between triumph and turmoil. Leading the race, Max suffered a tire blowout on the final lap, costing him a certain victory. The anguish in his eyes was palpable, a reflection of the highs and lows that defined his pursuit. Max's resilience, however, was unwavering. He channeled his disappointment into determination, a fire that burned brighter with each setback.

As the season progressed, Max continued to showcase his growth as a driver. He demonstrated a newfound understanding of race strategy, calculated risks, and the importance of consistency. The French Grand Prix victory was a sign of his maturity, a race where he expertly managed tire wear and maintained control under pressure.

The 2022 British Grand Prix reignited the rivalry with Lewis Hamilton. The Silverstone clash resulted in Max's car hurtling into the barriers, a collision that sent shockwaves through the sport. The incident ignited debates and discussions, highlighting the fine line between aggressive racing and dangerous maneuvers.

The challenges on the track were paralleled by the psychological warfare off it. Mind games, strategic maneuvers, and media exchanges became integral to the narrative. Max's interactions with the media demonstrated his evolution as a spokesperson for his sport. He engaged thoughtfully, combining candor with caution, aware of the power of his words.

Amidst the challenges, Max's determination to succeed burned brighter than ever. The Dutch Grand Prix at Zandvoort became a watershed moment. Racing in front of his home crowd, Max delivered a masterclass, securing victory and igniting celebrations that resonated far beyond the track. The triumph was not just a win; it was a demonstration of his unyielding spirit.

The 2022 United States Grand Prix showcased Max's refusal to yield to adversity. Starting from the back of the grid due to a power unit penalty, he executed a stunning comeback to finish second. It was a performance that showcased his ability to extract the maximum from any situation.

The final races of the 2022 season saw Max locked in a fierce title battle with Lewis Hamilton. The Saudi Arabian Grand Prix was emblematic of their rivalry, as they navigated a challenging street circuit under the desert lights. In a race marked by tension, Max secured a crucial victory, narrowing the championship gap.

As the season finale arrived in Abu Dhabi, the world watched with bated breath. The championship showdown went down to the wire, with Max and Lewis separated by a single point. The race unfolded in dramatic fashion, and Max's measured approach paid off. He clinched his first World Drivers' Championship title, a moment that marked the culmination of years of dedication, sacrifice, and unrelenting pursuit.

The chapter of challenges and setbacks was a testament to Max Verstappen's unwavering commitment to his dream. The victories were sweeter because of the obstacles he had overcome, and the setbacks had only fueled his fire. Max's journey from karting sensation to

Formula One world champion was not just a triumph of skill.

As the confetti rained down on the podium in Abu Dhabi, Max held the championship trophy aloft. The echoes of his battles, his triumphs, and his setbacks reverberated through the paddock, a reminder that the path to greatness was paved with challenges that ultimately defined his legacy.

Chapter 9: Max Verstappen's Driving Style

Max Verstappen's journey to becoming a Formula One world champion was not solely defined by his victories and challenges; his distinct and aggressive driving style played a pivotal role. From his audacious overtakes to his calculated risk-taking, Max's approach on the track set him apart as a formidable force. In this chapter, we delve into the intricacies of Max's driving style, examining his braking techniques, cornering finesse, and his unique approach to tire management. We also gain insights from engineers, teammates, and rivals who have had the firsthand experience of racing against the Dutch prodigy.

Max Verstappen's braking prowess is a cornerstone of his driving style. His ability to brake later than his competitors while maintaining control is a indication to his extraordinary car control and spatial awareness. According to his race engineers, Max's intuitive understanding of braking points and tire grip allows him to exploit the limits of deceleration, gaining precious milliseconds that can be the difference between executing an overtake or falling behind.

Former teammate Daniel Ricciardo offered insights into Max's braking skills, acknowledging that his unwavering confidence in late braking often forced his rivals onto the defensive. "When racing against Max, you always knew he'd make a daring move at the braking zone. It added a psychological layer to defending against him," Ricciardo explained.

Max's approach to cornering merges precision with aggression. His capability to maintain speed through corners while adhering to a consistent racing line is pivotal in creating overtaking opportunities on exits. Peers who have raced alongside him have consistently lauded his racecraft during intense battles. Sergio Perez, Max's current teammate at Red Bull Racing, commented, "Being on the same team as Max highlights his impeccable car control, particularly in tight situations. His adeptness at positioning the car and maintaining control through corners is exceptional."

Jos Verstappen, Max's father and a keen observer of his career, emphasized his son's prowess in corner exits. "Max's emphasis on corner exits sets him apart. He can get on the throttle early, efficiently harnessing the car's grip. This skill is what makes him formidable in wheel-to-wheel combat," Jos remarked.

Verstappen's driving style is a symphony of split-second decisions and deft car control. His ability to change direction with unparalleled speed through complex corners like Maggots and Becketts at Silverstone has left seasoned observers astounded. Peter Windsor, a seasoned Formula One journalist, captured the essence of Verstappen's approach, highlighting his capacity to create an infinitesimal "flat area" between directional changes. This micro-momentary equilibrium allows him to maintain a stable balance with the car, ensuring a seamless transition between steering and throttle inputs.

Max's driving style extends to his mastery of tire management, a pivotal aspect of Formula One racing. His capability to balance performance extraction with tire preservation has been instrumental in his triumphs. Engineers at Red Bull Racing have commended Max for his comprehensive feedback on tire behavior, enabling the team to refine strategies mid-race. Max's adaptability in altering his driving style to accommodate tire wear underscores his profound technical understanding.

Teammate Sergio Perez offered insights into Max's tire management approach, explaining, "Max possesses a unique ability to push hard while still maintaining tire longevity. It's a talent that stems from his comprehension of the equilibrium between aggressive driving and preservation."

Insights from Spectators

Eddie Irvine, a former Formula One driver, lauds Verstappen as the epitome of a team leader's dominance. Acknowledging his role as the focal point of Red Bull Racing, Irvine underscores that Verstappen's teammates have been unable to bridge the chasm he creates. The stark contrast in performance against teammates underscores his unassailable position as the true leader of his team.

Jenson Button's assertion during the 2020 season that Verstappen's annihilation of his teammates is unparalleled resonates to show his level of supremacy. In a sport defined by fierce competition. Niki Lauda's proclamation of Verstappen as the "talent of the century" after his maiden Formula One win at the 2016 Spanish Grand Prix resonated with the sentiments of many.

Christian Horner's words, labeling Verstappen as the best driver ever seen in Red Bull colors, underscored the magnitude of his impact on the team. The assertion that he embodies the pinnacle of raw ability and commitment elevates Verstappen's stature beyond mere statistics.

Gerhard Berger's endorsement of Verstappen as the era's most talented driver was a nod to his unparalleled gifts. The acknowledgment that raw talent is merely a component of the entire package speaks volumes about the well-rounded excellence Verstappen brings to the track.

Fernando Alonso's assertion that Verstappen is "one step ahead" of his peers highlights his exceptional edge. As the battles raged on, Verstappen consistently demonstrated a level of mastery that extended beyond the boundaries of his car's performance.

Karun Chandhok's comparison of Verstappen's combativeness to the legendary Michael Schumacher reflects the audacious spirit that defines Verstappen's approach. His relentless pursuit of victory, combined with his unwavering determination, paints a picture of a driver unyielding in the face of challenges.

As the 2021 season unfurled, Motorsport columnist Jolyon Palmer foresaw a new era of dominance emerging. He deciphered Verstappen's mastery by dissecting his qualifying pace, a hallmark of his championship campaign. Verstappen's pole positions stood as a testimony to his skill to extract the maximum from his car, often reaching a level of sheer perfection that left his rivals in awe.

Journalist Scott Mitchell's analysis delved deeper into the mystique of Verstappen's prowess. Mitchell unveiled the enigma that lies in his intuitive driving style. Verstappen's capacity to drive on intuition, honed through years of training, separates him from the rest. The "database in his head" allows him to channel his intuition into instantaneous actions, making his style virtually impossible to replicate.

Helmut Marko's insights added another layer to Verstappen's dominance. Marko's comparison with former teammate Daniel Ricciardo showcased Verstappen's progression. The data-driven assessment revealed Verstappen's uncanny ability to manage his tires even when his car slides more, leaving competitors trailing in his wake.

In essence, Verstappen's driving style transcends mere wins and losses. It embodies raw talent, unparalleled commitment, and an intuitive understanding of the track. His era of excellence stands to his show unique ability to captivate spectators and experts alike, solidifying his place in Formula One history.

Chapter 10: Off-Court Contributions

Max Verstappen's influence extends beyond the racetrack, reaching into realms that underscore his role as not just a driver, but a global icon. This chapter delves into the significant off-court contributions he has made, demonstrating his commitment to societal impact, safety advocacy, and environmental consciousness.

Max Verstappen's dedication to safety extends beyond his own well-being on the track. He actively participates in campaigns and initiatives geared towards enhancing safety standards within Formula One and motorsport at large. His engagement in the development of safety protocols, the evolution of car design, and the implementation of driver protection mechanisms highlights his recognition of the broader responsibilities that come with his stature.

Verstappen's involvement in safety campaigns serves as an exemplar for both established racers and budding talents. His ability to merge his prominence with the betterment of the sport underscores his role as a mentor, setting the tone for responsible racing that places safety at the forefront.

Max Verstappen's commitment to environmental consciousness is a manifestation of his recognition of the world's broader challenges. He employs his platform to champion sustainability, encouraging a shift towards responsible practices within motorsport and beyond.Through his actions and statements, Verstappen underscores the importance of embracing renewable energy, efficient resource usage, and environmental awareness. His role as a vocal advocate for sustainability serves as an inspiration for fans, urging them to consider the environmental impact of their choices.

Max Verstappen's philanthropic initiatives exemplify his aspiration to leverage his influence for the betterment of society. The Max Verstappen Foundation, established to support various charitable causes, highlights his dedication to assisting those in need. The foundation's initiatives, ranging from aiding children's hospitals to supporting underprivileged communities, showcase Verstappen's empathy and his desire to create positive change beyond the racetrack. His contributions stand as a prove to the notion that success should be a catalyst for making the world a better place.

Max Verstappen's off-court endeavors are an embodiment of his recognition that his reach extends far beyond the Formula One paddock. He understands the potential he holds to inspire younger generations, not just in motorsport but in the realm of life choices and values. Through his engagements, public appearances, and online interactions, Verstappen crafts a relatable image that resonates with the youth. His journey from a young karting prodigy to a Formula One world champion.

Beyond being a remarkable driver, he embodies a multifaceted persona that wields his prominence for positive change. His involvement in safety initiatives, commitment to environmental sustainability, philanthropic endeavors, and inspirational influence on the youth amplify his legacy beyond trophies and titles. Max Verstappen's legacy is one that underscores the profound impact an individual can have when they choose to wield their influence for the greater good.

Max Verstappen: A Biography

Chapter 11: Legacy and Future

Max Verstappen's journey through the fast-paced world of Formula One has left an indelible mark that extends far beyond the racetrack. As he continues to navigate his path, his legacy expands while his future holds the promise of fresh accomplishments and novel challenges. This chapter delves into the enduring legacy he has already forged and explores the potential avenues that his journey may lead him down.

Max Verstappen's legacy is not confined to the realm of victories and championship titles. He has emerged as a symbol of tenacity, resilience, and sportsmanship, his journey serving as a beacon of inspiration for aspiring racers across the globe. Through the unwavering blend of determination, raw talent, and tireless effort, he exemplifies the transformation of dreams into tangible reality.

Central to Max's legacy is his commitment to giving back. His active participation in safety initiatives and his passionate advocacy for environmental sustainability underscore his aspiration to harness his influence for positive transformation. Evident through the establishment of the Max Verstappen Foundation, aimed at supporting various charitable endeavors.

Max's legacy is also about his role in widening the audience of Formula One. His captivating style of racing, his engaging demeanor off the track, and his interactions with fans have garnered him a worldwide following. The passionate "Orange Army" of Dutch supporters rallying behind him during races signifies his ability to unify individuals under a shared banner of enthusiasm.

As Max Verstappen's journey continues, his trajectory in Formula One is replete with both opportunities and challenges. He remains a linchpin within the Red Bull Racing team, at the forefront of their quest to achieve supremacy against formidable adversaries. The ongoing rivalry with Lewis Hamilton promises to keep the excitement palpable in the upcoming seasons, captivating audiences worldwide with their breathtaking battles.

The pursuit of additional championships stands as a beacon on Max's horizon. The prospect of ascending to the ranks of multiple-time world champions looms large, and his commitment to pushing the boundaries of his abilities remains unwavering. His experiences, triumphs, and lessons absorbed throughout his journey will undoubtedly serve as the compass guiding his approach to forthcoming seasons.

Max's evolution as a racer is a dynamic continuum, and as he refines his skills, his potential to act as a mentor and inspiration for the next generation of drivers grows in significance. His role as a mentor could prove as impactful as his triumphs on the track. Sharing his insights and experiences has the potential to shape the future of Formula One, nurturing budding talents and shepherding them through the intricate landscape of motorsport.

Beyond the racetrack, Max's contributions in the spheres of safety, sustainability, and philanthropy stand poised for expansion. His status as a world champion endows him with the power to amplify his impact and advocate for positive transformation within the sport and beyond. His endeavors stand as a resounding prove to the proposition that athletes can wield their influence to catalyze positive change within society.

Max Verstappen's legacy is a mosaic woven from strands of fervor, fortitude, and an unwavering pursuit of perfection. His voyage

from a karting prodigy to a Formula One world
champion has been a journey marked by
victories, obstacles, and an inexorable
commitment to leaving a constructive imprint
on the world. His legacy reverberates beyond
mere trophies, resonating within the hearts and
minds of admirers, fellow competitors, and
those touched by his philanthropic initiatives.

As the path before him unfurls, Max's future
holds the promise of additional triumphs,
championship quests, and an ongoing impact on
the sport. His expedition remains a narrative in
progression, with each race and every season
appending fresh chapters to a story that has held
the motorsport world captive. Max Verstappen's
legacy is an indicator to the potential of ardor,
perseverance, and the unending pursuit of
magnificence, setting the stage for a future that
is brimming with boundless potential.

Max Verstappen: A Biography

Printed in Great Britain
by Amazon